THE STILL HOUR

THE STILL HOUR

or

Communion With God

AUSTIN PHELPS

'He that dwelleth in the secret place of the most High shall abide under the shadow of the Almighty.'—PSALM 91:1.

THE BANNER OF TRUTH TRUST

THE BANNER OF TRUTH TRUST
3 Murrayfield Road, Edinburgh EH12 6EL
P.O. Box 652, Carlisle, Pennsylvania 17013, USA

*

First published in U.S.A. in 1859
First Banner of Truth Trust
reprint 1974

ISBN 0 85151 202 X

*

Printed and bound in Great Britain
by Hazell Watson & Viney Ltd,
Aylesbury, Bucks

PREFATORY NOTE

Some subjects of religious meditation are always timely, and *standard* thoughts upon them the most timely. Such, it is hoped, will be found to be the character of the following pages.

A portion of them has been delivered as a sermon, in the Chapel of the Andover Theological Seminary, and several times elsewhere. Evidences of their usefulness in that form have been so obvious, that the author is induced to comply with the repeated requests which have reached him that they should be given to the press.

That they should be much enlarged in the course of revision for this purpose, is almost the necessary result of a review of a subject so prolific, and so vital to Christian hearts.

Contents

1: ABSENCE OF GOD IN PRAYER

'Oh that I knew where I might find him!' – Job 23:3

'If God had not said, "Blessed are those that hunger," I know not what could keep weak Christians from sinking in despair. Many times, all I can do is to complain that I want Him, and wish to recover Him.'

Bishop Hall, in uttering this lament two centuries and a half ago, only echoed the wail which had come down, through living hearts, from the patriarch, whose story is the oldest known literature in any language. A consciousness of the *absence of God* is one of the standard incidents of religious life. Even when the forms of devotion are observed conscientiously, the sense of the presence of God, as an invisible friend, whose society is a joy, is by no means unintermittent.

The truth of this will not be questioned by one who is familiar with those phases of religious experience which are so often the burden of Christian confession. In no single feature of 'inner life,' probably, is the experience of many minds less satisfactory to them than in this. They seem to themselves, in prayer, to have little, if any, effluent emotion. They can speak of little in their devotional life that seems to them *like* life; of little that appears like the communion of a living soul with a living God. Are there not many 'closet hours,' in which the chief feeling of the worshipper is an oppressed consciousness of the absence of reality from his own exercises? He has no words which are, as George Herbert says, 'heart deep.' He not only experiences no ecstasy, but no joy, no peace, no repose. He has no sense of being at home with God. The stillness of the hour is the stillness of a dead calm at sea. The heart rocks monotonously on the surface of the great thoughts of God, of Christ, of eternity, of heaven—

> *As idle as a painted ship*
> *Upon a painted ocean.*

Such experiences in prayer are often startling in the contrast with those of certain Christians, whose communion with God, as the hints of it are recorded in their biographies, seems to realize, in actual being, the scriptural conception of a life which is hid with Christ in God.

We read of Payson, that his mind, at times, almost lost its sense of the external world, in the ineffable thoughts of God's glory, which rolled like a sea of light around him at the throne of grace.

We read in Cowper, that in one of the few lucid hours of his religious life, such was the experience of God's presence which he enjoyed in prayer, that, as he tells us, he thought he should have died with joy, if special strength had not been imparted to him to bear the disclosure.

We read of one of the Tennents, that on one occasion, when he was engaged in secret devotion, so overpowering was the revelation of God which opened upon his soul, and with augmenting intensity of effulgence as he prayed, that at length he recoiled from the intolerable joy as from a pain, and besought God to withhold from him further manifestations of His glory. He said, 'Shall thy servant *see* thee and live?'

We read of the 'sweet hours' which Edwards enjoyed 'on the banks of Hudson's River, in secret converse with God'; and hear his own description of the inward sense of Christ which at times came into his heart, and which he 'knows not how to express otherwise than by a calm, sweet abstraction of soul from all the concerns of this world; and sometimes a kind of vision . . . of being alone in the mountains, or some solitary wilderness, far from all mankind, sweetly conversing with Christ, and rapt and swallowed up in God.'

We read of such instances of the fruits of prayer, in the blessedness of the suppliant, and are we not reminded by them of the transfiguration of our Lord, of whom we read, 'As he prayed, the fashion of his countenance was altered, and his raiment became white and glistering'? Who of us is not oppressed by the contrast between such an experience and his own? Does not the cry of the patriarch come unbidden to our lips, 'Oh that I knew where *I* might find him?'

Much of even the ordinary language of Christians, respecting the joy of communion with God, – language which is stereotyped in our dialect of prayer – many cannot honestly apply to the history of their own minds. A calm, fearless self-examination finds no counterpart to it in anything they have ever known. In the view of an honest conscience, it is not the vernacular speech of their experience. As compared with the joy which such language indicates, prayer is, in all that they know of it, a dull duty. Perhaps the characteristic of the feelings of many about it is expressed in the single fact, that it *is* to them a duty as distinct from a privilege. It is a duty which, they cannot deny, is often uninviting, even irksome.

If some of us should attempt to define the advantage we derive from a performance of the duty, we might be surprised, perhaps shocked, as one after another of the folds of a deceived heart should be taken off, at the discovery of the littleness of the residuum, in an honest judgment of ourselves. Why did we pray this morning? Do we often derive any other profit from prayer, than that of satisfying convictions of conscience, of which we could not rid ourselves if we wished to do so, and which will not permit us to be at ease with ourselves, if all forms of prayer are abandoned? Perhaps even so slight a thing as the pain of resistance to the momentum of a habit will be found to be the most distinct reason we can honestly give for having prayed yesterday or to-day.

There may be periods, also, when the experiences of the closet enable some of us to understand that maniacal cry of Cowper, when his friends requested him to prepare some hymns for the Olney Collection: 'How can you ask of me such a service? I seem to myself to be banished to a remoteness from God's presence, in comparison with which the distance from east to west is vicinity, is cohesion.'

If such language is too strong to be truthful to the common experience of the class of professing Christians to which those whom it represents belong, many will still discern in it, as an expression of joylessness in prayer, a sufficient approximation of their own experience, to awaken interest in some thoughts upon the *causes of a want of enjoyment in prayer*.

The evil of such an experience in prayer is too obvious to need illustration. If any light can be thrown upon the causes of it, there is no man living, whatever may be his religious state, who has not an interest in making it the theme of inquiry. 'Never any more wonder,' says an old writer, 'that men pray so seldom. For there are

[13]

very few that feel the *relish*, and are enticed with the *deliciousness*, and refreshed with the *comforts*, and acquainted with the *secrets*, of a holy prayer.' Yet, who is it that has said, 'I will make them *joyful* in my house of prayer'?

2: UNHALLOWED PRAYER

'What is the hope of the hypocrite? Will God hear his cry?' – JOB 27:8, 9

An impenitent sinner never prays. In an inquiry after the causes of joylessness in the forms of prayer, the very first which meets us, in some instances, is the *absence of piety*. It is useless to search behind or beneath such a cause as this for a more recondite explanation of the evil. This is, doubtless, often all the interpretation that can be honestly given to a man's experience in addressing God. Other reasons for the lifelessness of his soul in prayer are rooted in this – that he is not a Christian.

If the heart is not right with God, enjoyment of communion with God is impossible. That communion itself is impossible. I repeat, an impenitent sinner never prays. Impenitence involves not one of the elements of a spirit of prayer. Holy desire, holy love, holy fear, holy trust – not one of these can the sinner find within himself. He has, therefore, none of that artless spontaneity, in calling upon God, which David exhibited when he said, 'Thy servant hath *found in his heart* to pray this prayer unto thee.' An impenitent sinner finds no such thing in *his* heart. He finds there no intelligent wish to enjoy God's friendship. The whole atmosphere of prayer, therefore, is foreign to his tastes. If he drives himself into it for a time,

[15]

by forcing upon his soul the forms of devotion, he cannot stay there. He is like one gasping in a vacuum.

One of the most impressive mysteries of the condition of man on this earth, is his deprivation of all visible and audible representations of God. We seem to be living in a state of seclusion from the rest of the universe, and from that peculiar presence of God in which angels dwell, and in which departed saints serve Him day and night. We do not see Him in the fire; we do not hear Him in the wind; we do not feel Him in the darkness. But a more awful concealment of God from the unregenerate soul exists by the very law of an unregenerate state. The eye of such a soul is closed even upon the spiritual manifestations of God, in all but their retributive aspects. These are all that it feels. These are all the thoughts of God which it has faith in. Such a soul does not enjoy God, for it does not see God with an eye of *faith* – that is, as a living God, living close to itself, and in vital relations to its own destiny – except as a retributive Power.

The only thing that forbids life, in any of its experiences, to be a life of retribution to an impenitent sinner, is a dead sleep of moral insensibility. And this sleep cannot be disturbed while he remains impenitent, otherwise than by disclosures of God as a consuming fire. His experience, therefore, in the forms of devotion, while he abides in impenitence, can only vibrate between the extremes of weariness and of terror. Quell his fear of God, and prayer becomes irksome; stimulate his indifference to God, and prayer becomes a torment.

The notes of a flute are sometimes a torture to the ears of idiots, like the blare of a trumpet. The reason has been conjectured to be, that melodious sound unlocks the tomb of idiotic mind by the suggestion of conceptions, dim, but startling, like a revelation of a higher life, with which that mind has certain crushed affinities, but with which it feels no willing sympathy; so that its own degradation, disclosed to it by the contrast, is seated upon the consciousness of idiocy like a nightmare. Such a stimulant only to suffering may the form of prayer be in the experience of sin. Impenitent prayer can only grovel in stagnant sensibility, or agonize in remorseful torture, or oscillate from one to the other. There is no point of joy between to which it can gravitate, and there rest.

It is not wise that even we, who profess to be followers of Christ, should close our eyes to this truth, that the uniform absence of joy in prayer is one of the threatening signs in respect of our religious state. It is one of the legitimate intimations of that estrangement from God, which sin induces in one who has not experienced God's renewing grace. A searching of ourselves with an honest desire to know the truth, and the whole of it, may disclose to us other kindred facts, *with* which this feature of our condition becomes reasonable evidence, which it will be the loss of our souls to neglect, that we are self-deluded in our Christian hope. An apostle might number us among the 'many,' of whom he would say, 'I now tell you, even weeping, that they are enemies of the cross of Christ.'

3: ROMANCE IN PRAYER

'If I regard iniquity in my heart, the Lord will not hear me.'—Psa. 66:18

We often affront God by offering prayers which we are not *willing* to have answered. Theoretical piety is never more deceptive than in acts of devotion. We pray for blessings which we know to be accordant with God's will, and we persuade ourselves that we desire those blessings. In the abstract, we do desire them. A sane mind must be far gone in sympathy with devils, if it can help desiring all virtue in the abstract.

The *dialect* of prayer established in Christian usage wins our trust; we sympathize with its theoretical significance; we find no fault with its intensity of spiritual life. It commends itself to our conscience and good sense, as being what the phraseology of devout affection should be. Ancient forms of prayer are beautiful exceedingly. Their hallowed associations fascinate us like old songs. In certain imaginative moods we fall into delicious reverie over them. Yet down deep in our heart of hearts we may detect more of poetry than of piety in this fashion of joy. We are troubled, therefore, and our countenance is changed.

Many of the prime objects of prayer enchant us only in the distance. Brought near to us, and in concrete forms, and made to grow lifelike in our conceptions, they very sensibly abate the pulse of our longing to possess them, because we cannot but discover that, to realize them in our lives, certain other darling objects must be sacrificed, which we are not yet willing to part with. The paradox is true to the life, that a man may even *fear* an answer to his prayers.

A very good *devotee* may be a very dishonest suppliant. When he leaves the height of meditative abstraction, and, as we very significantly say in our Saxon phrase, *comes to himself*, he may find that his true character, his *real* self, is that of no petitioner at all. His devotions have been dramatic. The sublimities of the closet have been but illusions. He has been acting a pantomime. He has not really desired that God would give heed to him, for any other purpose than to give him an hour of pleasurable devotional excitement. That his objects of prayer should actually be inwrought into his character, and should live in his own consciousness, is by no means the thing he has been thinking of, and is the last thing he is ready just now to wish for. If he has a Christian heart buried anywhere beneath this heap of pietism, it is very probable that the discovery of the burlesque of prayer of which he has been guilty, will transform his fit of romance into some sort of hypochondriacal suffering. Despondency is the natural offspring of theatrical devotion.

Let us observe this paradox of Christian life in two or three illustrations.

An *envious* Christian – we must tolerate the contradiction; to be true to the facts of life we must join strange opposites – an envious Christian prays, with becoming devoutness, that God will impart to him a generous, loving spirit, and a conscience void of offence to all men. His mind is in a solemn state, his heart is not insensible to the beauty of the virtues which he seeks. His posture is lowly, his tones sincere, and self-delusion is one of these processes of weakness which are facilitated by the deception of bodily habitude. His prayer goes on glibly, till conscience grows impatient, and reminds him of certain of his equals, whose prosperity stirs up within him that 'envy which is the rottenness of the bones.'

What then? Very probably he quits *that subject* of prayer, and passes to another, on which his conscience is not so eagle-eyed. But after that glimpse of a hidden sin, how do the clouds of estrangement from God seem to shut him in, dark and damp and chill, and his prayer become like a dismal pattering of rain!

An *ambitious* Christian prays that God will bestow upon him a humble spirit. He volunteers to take a low place because of his unworthiness. He asks that he may be delivered from pride and self-seeking. He repeats the prayer of the publican, and the benediction upon the poor in spirit. The whole group of the virtues kindred to humility seems to him as radiant as the graces with loveliness. He is sensible of no check in the fluency of his emotions, till *his* conscience, too, becomes angry and dashes the little eddy of goodness which is just now covering up the undertone of selfishness that imperils his soul. If then he is not melted into tears at the disclosure of his heartlessness, that prayer probably ends in a clouded brow, and a feverish, querulous self-conflict.

A *revengeful* Christian prays that he may have a meek spirit; that he may be harmless as doves; that the synonymous graces of forbearance, long-suffering, patience, may adorn his life; that he may put away bitterness, and wrath, and anger, and clamour, and evil-speaking, with all malice; that that mind may be found in him which was also in Christ. At the moment of this devotional episode in his experience, he feels, as Rousseau did, the abstract grandeur of a magnanimity like that of Jesus. There is no doubt about the fervour of his theoretic love of such an ideal of character; and he is about to take courage from his rapture, when his conscience becomes impertinent, and mocks him, by thrusting upon his lips the words which are death to his conceit – 'Forgive me *as* I forgive.' If then he is not shocked into self-abhorrence at the ghastliness of his guilt, he probably exhausts that hour of prayer in palliations and compromises, or in reckless impositions upon the forbearance of God.

A *luxurious* Christian prays, in the good set phrases of devotion, for a spirit of self-denial; that he may endure hardness as a good soldier of Christ; that he may take up the cross and follow Christ; that he may be ready to forsake all that he hath, and be Christ's disciple; that he may not live unto himself; that he may imitate Him who went about doing good – who became poor that we might be rich, and who wept over lost souls. In such a prayer there may be, consciously, no insincerity, but a pleasureable sympathy, rather, with the grand thoughts and the grander feeling which the language portrays. The heart is buoyant with its gaseous distension to the bounds of its great swelling words.

This lover of the pride of life does not discover his self-inflation, till conscience pricks him with such goads as these: 'Are you living for the things you are praying for?' 'What one thing are you doing for Christ which costs you self-denial?' 'Are you *seeking* for opportunities to deny yourself, to save souls?' 'Are you willing to be *like* Him who had not where to lay his head?' 'Can you be baptized with the baptism that He was baptized with?' If, then, this effeminate one is not roused to a more Christ-like life by the uncovering of his hypocrisy, what a sickly murmuring of self-reproach fills his heart at the collapse of that prayer!

Such is human nature; such, but by the grace of

God, are we all. We must be dull inspectors of our own hearts, if we have never discerned there, lurking *beneath* the level at which sin breaks out into overt crime, some single offence – an offence of feeling, an offence of habit in thought, which for a time has spread its infection over the whole character of our devotions. We have been self-convicted of falsehood in prayer; for, though praying in the full dress of sound words, we did not desire that our supplications should be heard at the expense of that one idol.

Perhaps that single sin has woven itself like a web over large spaces of our life. It may have run like a shuttle to and fro in the texture of some plan of life, on which our conscience has not glared fiercely as upon a crime, because the usage of the world has blindfolded conscience by the respectability of such sin. Yet it has been all the while tightening its folds around us, repressing our liberty in prayer, stopping the life-blood and weakening the fibre of our moral being, till we are like kneeling corpses in our worship.

That is a deceptive notion which attributes the want of unction in prayer to an arbitrary, or even inexplicable withdrawment of God from the soul. Aside from the operation of physical causes, where is the warrant, in reason or revelation, for ascribing joylessness in prayer to *any* other cause than some wrong in the soul itself? What an old prophet? 'Behold, the Lord's ear is *not* heavy that it cannot hear; but your *iniquities* have separated between you and your God. Your *sins* have hid his face from you. *Therefore*, we wait for light, but behold obscurity; for brightness, but we walk in darkness. We grope for the wall like the blind; we grope as if we had no eyes: we stumble at noonday as in the night; we are in desolate places as dead men.' Could words describe more truthfully, or explain more philosophically, that phenomenon of religious experience which we call the 'hiding of God's countenance'?

It does not require what the world pronounces a *great* sin, to break up the serenity of the soul in its devotional hours. The experience of prayer has delicate complications. A little thing, secreted there, may dislocate its mechanism and arrest its movement. The spirit of prayer is to the soul what the eye is to the body, – the eye, so limpid in its nature, of such fine finish and such intricate convolution in its structure, and of so sensitive nerve, that the point of a needle may excruciate it, and make it weep itself away.

Even a *doubtful* principle of life, harboured in the heart, is perilous to the peacefulness of devotion. May not many of us find the cause of our joylessness in prayer, in the fact that we are living upon some *unsettled principles* of conduct? We are assuming the rectitude of courses of life with which we are not ourselves honestly satisfied.

I apprehend that there is very much of *suspense* of conscience among Christians upon subjects of practical life, on which there is no suspense of *action*. Is there not a pretty large cloud-land covered by the usages of Christian society? And may not some of us find *there* the sin which infects our devotions with nauseous incense?

Possibly our hearts are shockingly deceitful in such iniquity. Are we strangers to an experience like this – that when we mourn over our cold prayers as a misfortune, we evade a search of that disputed territory for the cause of them, through fear that we shall find it there, and we struggle to satisfy ourselves with an increase of spiritual duties which shall cost us no sacrifice? Are we never sensible of resisting the hints which the Holy Spirit gives us in parables, by refusing to *look that way* for the secret of our deadness – saying, 'Not that! Oh no, not that! But let us *pray* more?'

Many a doubtful principle in a Christian mind, if once set in the focus of a conscience illumined by the Holy Spirit, would resolve itself into a sin, for which that Christian would turn and look up guilty to the Master, and then go out and weep bitterly.

4: DISTRUST IN PRAYER

'What profit should we have, if we pray unto him?' —
JOB 21:15

The great majority of us have little *faith* in
prayer. This is one of those causes which may
produce a habit of mind in devotion resembling
that of impenitent prayer, and yet distinguish-
able from it, and co-existent, often, with some
degree of genuine piety. Christians often have
little faith in prayer as a *power in real life*. They
do not embrace cordially, in feeling as well as in
theory, the truth which underlies the entire
spiritual conception and illustration of prayer,
that it is literally, actually, positively, effectually,
a means of power.

Singular as it may appear, the fact is indisput-
able, that Christian practice is often at a dis-
count by the side of heathen habits of devotion.
Heathen prayer, whatever else it is or is not, is a
reality in the heathen idea. A pagan suppliant
has faith in prayer, as he understands it. Grovel-
ling as his notion of it is, such as it is he *means* it.
He trusts it as an instrument of power. He
expects to accomplish something by praying.

When Ethelfrith, the Saxon king of Northum-
bria, invaded Wales, and was about to give battle
to the Britons, he observed near the enemy
a host of unarmed men. He enquired who they
were, and what they were doing. He was told

that they were monks of Bangor, praying for the success of their countrymen. 'Then,' said the heathen prince, 'they have begun the *fight* against us; attack them *first*.'

So any unperverted mind will conceive of the scriptural idea of prayer, as that of one of the most downright, sturdy realities in the universe. Right in the heart of God's plan of government it is lodged as a power. Amidst the conflicts which are going on in the evolution of that plan, it stands as a power. Into all the intricacies of divine working and the mysteries of divine decree, it reaches out silently as a power. In the mind of God, we may be assured, the conception of prayer is no fiction, whatever man may think of it.

It has, and God has *determined* that it should have, a positive and an appreciable influence in directing the course of a human life. It is, and God has *purposed* that it should be, a link of connection between human mind and divine mind, by which, through His infinite condescension, we may actually move His will. It is, and God has *decreed* that it should be, a *power* in the universe, as distinct, as real, as natural, and as uniform, as the power of gravitation, or of light, or of electricity. A man may *use* it as trustingly and as soberly as he would use any of these. It is as truly the dictate of good sense that a man should expect to achieve something by praying, as it is that he should expect to achieve something by a telescope, or the mariner's compass, or the electric telegraph.

This intense practicalness characterizes the scriptural idea of prayer. The Scriptures make it a reality, and not a reverie. They never bury it in the notion of a poetic or philosophic contemplation of God. They do not merge it in the mental fiction of prayer by action in any other or all other duties of life. They have not concealed the fact of prayer beneath the mystery of prayer. The scriptural utterances on the subject of prayer admit of no such reduction of tone and confusion of sense as men often put forth in imitating them. Up, on the level of inspired thought, *prayer is* PRAYER – a distinct, unique, elemental power in the spiritual universe, as pervasive and as constant as the great hidden powers of Nature.

The want of trust in this scriptural ideal of prayer often neutralizes it, even in the experience of a Christian. The result cannot be otherwise. It lies in the nature of mind.

Observe, for a moment, the philosophy of this. Mind is so made that it needs the hope of *gaining an object*, as an inducement to effort. Even so simple an effort as that involved in the utterance of desire, no man will make persistently, with no hope of gaining an object. Despair of an object is speechless. So, if you wish to enjoy prayer, you must first form to yourself such a theory of prayer – or, if you do not consciously form it, you must *have* it – and then you must cherish such trust in it, as a reality, that you shall feel the force of an object in prayer. No mind can feel that it has object in praying, except in such degree as it appreciates the scriptural view of prayer as a genuine thing.

Our conviction on this point must be as definite and as fixed as our trust in the evidence of our senses. It must become as natural to us to obey one as the other. If we suffer our faith to drop down from the lofty conception of prayer as having a lodgment in the very counsels of God, by which the universe is swayed, the plain practicalness of prayer, as the Scriptures teach it, and as the prophets and apostles and our Lord Himself performed it, drops proportionately; and in that proportion our motive to prayer dwindles. Of necessity, then, our devotions become spiritless. We cannot obey such faith in prayer, with any more heart than a man who is afflicted with double vision can feel in obeying the evidence of his eyes. Our supplications cannot, under the impulse of such a faith, go, as one has expressed it, 'in a right line to God.' They become circuitous, timid, heartless. They may so degenerate as to be offensive, 'like the reekings of the Dead Sea.'

5: FAITH IN PRAYER

'As a prince hast thou power with God.' – GEN. 32:28

An intrepid faith in prayer will always give it unction. Let the faith of apostles in the reality of prayer as a power with God take possession of a regenerate heart, and it is inconceivable that prayer should be to that heart a lifeless *duty*. The joy of hope, at least, will vitalize the duty. The prospect of gaining an object will always affect thus the expression of intense desire.

The feeling which will become spontaneous with a Christian, under the influence of such a trust, is this: 'I come to my devotions this morning, on an errand of real life. This is no romance and no farce. I do not come here to go through a form of words. I have no hopeless desires to express. I have an object to gain. I have an end to accomplish. This is a *business* in which I am about to engage. An astronomer does not turn his telescope to the skies with a more reasonable hope of penetrating those distant heavens, than I have of reaching the mind of God, by lifting up my heart at the throne of grace. This is the privilege of my calling of God in Christ Jesus. Even my faltering voice is now to be heard in heaven, and it is to put forth a power there, the results of which only God can know, and only eternity can develop. "Therefore, O

Lord, thy servant findeth it in his heart to pray this prayer unto thee.''

'Good prayers,' says an old English divine, 'never come weeping home. I am sure I shall receive either what I ask or what I should ask.' Such a habit of feeling as this will give to prayer that quality which Dr. Chalmers observed as being the characteristic of the prayers of Doddridge – that they had an intensely 'business-like' spirit.

Observe how thoroughly this spirit is infused into the scriptural representation of the interior working of prayer in the counsels of God, respecting the prophet Daniel. The narrative is intelligible to a child; yet scarcely another passage in the Bible is so remarkable, in its bearing upon the difficulties which our minds often generate out of the mystery of prayer. Almost the very mechanism of the plan of God, by which this invisible power enters into the execution of his decrees, is here laid open.

'Whiles I was speaking,' the prophet says, 'Gabriel, being caused to fly swiftly, touched me, and said, O Daniel, at the beginning of thy supplications, the commandment came forth, and I am come to shew thee; for thou art greatly beloved.' What greater vividness could be given to the reality of prayer, even to its hidden operation upon the divine decrees? No sooner do the words of supplication pass out from the lips, than

the command is given to one of the presence-
angels, 'Go thou'; and he flies swiftly to the
prostrate suppliant and touches him bodily, and
talks with him audibly, and assures him that his
desire is given to him. 'I am come to thee, O man
greatly beloved; I am commissioned to instruct
and to strengthen thee. I was delayed in my
journey to thee, else I had come more speedily to
thy relief. For one and twenty days the prince
of Persia withstood me; but Michael came to
help me, – the archangel is leagued with me to
execute the response to thy cry. _I_ must return to
fight that prince of Persia who would have restrained me from thee. Unto thee am I sent.
From the first day that thou didst set thy heart to
chasten thyself before thy God, thy words were
heard; and I am come because of thy words.
Again I say, O man greatly beloved, fear not.
Peace be unto thee; be strong, yea, be strong.'
Could any diagram of the working of prayer
amidst the purposes of God give to it a more vivid
reality in our conceptions, than it receives from
this little passage of dramatic narrative, which
you will find, in substance, in the ninth and
tenth chapters of the prophecy of Daniel?

I have sometimes tried to conceive a panorama
of the history of one prayer. I have endeavoured
to follow it from its inception in a human mind,
through its utterance by human lips; and in its
flight up to the ear of Him who is its Hearer,

because He has been also its Inspirer; and on its journey around to the unnumbered points in the organism of His decrees which this feeble human voice reaches, and from which it entices a responsive vibration, because this also is a decree of as venerable antiquity as theirs; and in its return from those altitudes, with its golden train of blessings to which eternal counsels have paid tribute, at His bidding. I have endeavoured to form some conception thus, of the methods by which this omnipotence of poor human speech gains its end, without a shock to the system of the universe, with not so much as a whit of change to the course of a leaf falling in the air. But how futile is the strain upon these puny faculties! How shadowy are the thoughts we get from any such attempt to *master* prayer! Do we not fall back with glad relief upon the magnitude of this *fact* of prayer, 'beyond the stars heard,' and answered through these ministries of angels?

Human art has now succeeded in extending the electric telegraph almost around our globe. But yonder is a child, whose lisping tongue is every day doing more than that. In God's administration of things, that child's morning prayer is a mightier reality than that. It sets in motion agencies more secret and more impalpable, and yet conscious agencies, whose chief vocation, so far as we know it, is to minister at that child's bidding: 'Verily I say unto you, that in heaven their angels do always behold the face of my Father who is in heaven.' Could we appreciate prayer, think you, as such a reality, such a power, so genuine, so vital a thing in the working of the divine plan, so free from trammel in its mystery, so much resembling the power of God *because* of its mystery, and yet could we find it to be in our own experience an insipid duty?

6: SPECIFIC AND INTENSE PRAYER

'As the hart panteth after the water brooks.' – Psa. 42:1

We lose many prayers for the want of two things which support each other, – *specificness of object* and *intensity of desire*. One's interest in such an exercise as this is necessarily dependent on the co-existence of these qualities.

In the diary of Dr. Chalmers, we find recorded this petition: 'Make me sensible of real answers to actual requests, as evidences of an interchange between myself on earth and my Saviour in heaven.' Under the sway of intense desires, our minds naturally long to individualize thus the parties, the petitions, the objects, and the results of prayer.

Sir Fowell Buxton writes as follows: 'When I am out of heart, I follow David's example, and fly for refuge to prayer; and he furnishes me with a store of prayer. . . . I am bound to acknowledge that I have always found that my prayers have been heard and answered; . . . in almost every instance I have received what I have asked for. . . . Hence, I feel permitted to offer up my prayers for everything that concerns me. I am inclined to imagine that there are no *little* things with God. His hand is as manifest in the feathers of a butterfly's wing, in the eye of an insect, in the folding and packing of a blossom, in the curious aqueducts by which a leaf is nourished, as in the

creation of a world, and in the laws by which
planets move. I understand literally the injunc-
tion: "In everything make your requests known
unto God"; and I cannot but notice how amply
these prayers have been met.'

Again, writing to his daughter on the subject of
a 'division' in the House of Commons, in the
conflict for West Indian Emancipation, he says:
'What led to that division? If ever there was a
subject which occupied our prayers, it was this.
Do you remember how we desired that God
would give me His Spirit in that emergency: how
we quoted the promise, "He that lacketh wisdom,
let him ask it of the Lord, and it *shall* be given
him"; and how I kept open that passage in the
Old Testament in which it is said, "We have no
might against this great company that cometh
against us, neither know we what to do, but our
eyes are upon Thee" – the Spirit of the Lord
replying, "Be not afraid nor dismayed by reason
of this great multitude, for the battle is not yours,
but God's"? If you want to see the passage, open
my Bible; it will turn of itself to the place. I
sincerely believe that *prayer* was the cause of
that division; and I am confirmed in this, by
knowing that we by no means calculated on the
effect. The course we took appeared to be right,
and we *followed it blindly*.'

In these examples is illustrated, in real life, the
working of these two forces in a spirit of prayer,

which must naturally exist or die together — intensity of desire and specificness of object.

Let a man define to his own mind an object of prayer, and then let him be moved by desires for that object which *impel* him to pray, because he cannot otherwise satisfy the irrepressible longings of his soul; let him have such desires as shall lead him to search out, and dwell upon, and treasure in his heart, and return to again, and appropriate to himself anew, the *encouragements* to prayer, till his Bible opens of itself at the right places — and think you that such a man will have occasion to go to his closet, or come from it, with the sickly cry, 'Why, oh! why is my intercourse with God so irksome to me?' Such a man *must* experience, at least, the joy of uttering hopefully emotions which become painful by repression.

On the contrary, let a man's objects of thought at the throne of grace be vague, and let his desires be languid, and, from the nature of the case, his prayers must be both languid and vague. Says Jeremy Taylor: 'Easiness of desire is a great enemy to the success of a good man's prayer. It must be an intent, zealous, busy, operative prayer. For consider what a huge indecency it is, that a man should speak to God for a thing that he values not. Our prayers upbraid our spirits, when we beg tamely for those things for which we ought to die; which are more precious than imperial sceptres, richer than the spoils of the sea, or the treasures of Indian hills.'

The scriptural examples of prayer have, most of them, an unutterable intensity. They are pictures of *struggles*, in which more of suppressed desire is hinted than that which is *ex*pressed. Recall the wrestling of Jacob – 'I will not let thee go till thou hast blest me'; and the 'panting' and 'pouring out of soul' of David – 'I cried day and night; my throat is dry with calling upon my God'; and the importunity of the Syro-Phœnician woman, with her 'Yes, Lord, yet the dogs under the table eat the children's crumbs'; and the persistency of Bartimaeus, crying out 'the more a great deal,' 'Have mercy on me'; and the strong crying and tears of our Lord – 'If it be possible! if it be possible!' There is no 'easiness of desire' here.

The scriptural examples of prayer, also, are clear as light in their objects of thought. Even those which are calm and sweet, like the Lord's Prayer, have few and sharply defined subjects of devotion. They are not discursive and volumin-ous, like many uninspired forms of supplication. They do not range over everything at once. They have no vague expressions; they are crystalline; a child need not read them a second time to understand them. As uttered by their authors, they were in no antiquated phraseology; they were in the fresh forms of a living speech. They

[39]

were. and were meant to be, the channels of living thoughts and living hearts.

Let a man, then, be negligent of both scriptural example and the nature of his own mind; let him approach God with both vagueness of thought and languor of emotion – and what else can his prayer be, but a weariness to himself and an abomination to God? It would be a miracle if such a suppliant should enjoy success in prayer. He cannot succeed, he cannot have joy, because he has no *object* that elicits intense desire, and no *desire* that sharpens his object. He has no great, holy, penetrative thought in him, which stirs up his sensibilities; and no deep, swelling sensibility, therefore, to *relieve* by prayer. His soul is not reached by anything he is thinking about; and, therefore, he *has* no soul to pour out before God. Such a man prays because he thinks he *must* pray; not because he is grateful to God that he *may* pray. There is an unspeakable difference between 'must' and 'may.' It is his conscience that prays; it is not his heart. His language is the language of his conscience. He prays in words which ought to express his heart, not in those which do express it. Hence arises that experience, so distressful to an ingenuous mind, in which devotion is prompted by no vividness of conception, rolling up a force of sensibility to the level of the lips, so that it *can* flow forth in childlike, honest speech.

Such an experience, so far from rendering

prayer a joy either sweet and placid or ecstatic, can only cause the time spent in the closet to be the season of periodical torture to a sensitive conscience, like that of a victim daily stretched on a rack. For it is in such prayer that such a conscience is most vehement in its reproaches, and guilt seems to be heaped up most rapidly. Oh, wretched man that he is! Who shall deliver him?

7: TEMPERAMENT OF PRAYER

'That disciple whom Jesus loved.' – JOHN 21:7

Some Christians do not cultivate the *temperament* of prayer. Devout joy is more facile to some temperaments than to others; yet, in all, it is susceptible of culture. Especially is it true that prayer is in its nature emotive. It is an expression of feeling; not necessarily of tumultuous feeling, but naturally of profound and fluent feeling, and, in its most perfect type, of habitual feeling. To enjoy prayer, we must be *used* to it. Therefore, we must be used to the sensibility of which it is the expression. Devotion should spring up spontaneously from an emotive *state*, rather than be forced out in jets of sensibility on great occasions.

The necessity of this is often overlooked by Christians whose lives, in other respects, are not visibly defective. They do not possess desires which may very naturally be expressed in prayer. They have no deep *subsoil* of feeling from which prayer would be a natural growth. The religion of some of us – whatever may be true of our opposites in temperament – is not sufficiently a religion of emotion. We have not sufficiently cherished our Christian sensibilities. We have not cultivated habits of religious desire which are buoyant in their working. We have not so trained our hearts, that a certain emotive current is always ebullient, welling up from the depths of the soul like the springs of the deepest sea. We think more than we believe. We believe more than we have faith in. Our faith is too calm, too cool, too sluggish. Our theory of the Christian life is that of a clear, erect, inflexible head, not of a great heart in which deep calleth unto deep.

This clear-headed type of piety has invaluable uses, if it be tempered with meekness, with gentleness, with 'bowels of mercies.' But we must confess that it does not always bear well the drill which the world gives it in selfish usage. It too often grows hard, solid, icy. It reminds one of the man with a 'cold heart,' whose blood never ran warm, whose eye was always glassy, whose touch was always clammy, and whose breath was always like an east wind. Such a religious temperament as this will never do for the foundation of a life of joy in communion with God. We must have more of the earnest nature of the loved disciple, more of the spirit of the visions of Patmos.

Our Northern and Occidental constitution often needs to be restrained from an excess of phlegmatic wisdom. I must think that we have something to learn from the more impulsive working of the Southern and the Oriental mind. I must believe that it was not without a wise forecast of the world's necessities, and an insight into human nature *all around*, that God ordained that the Bible, which should contain our best models of sanctified culture, should be constructed in the East, and by the inspiration of minds of an Eastern stock and discipline, whose imaginative faculty could conceive such a poem as the Song of Solomon, and whose emotive nature could be broken up like the fountains of a great deep. I must anticipate that an improved symmetry of character will be imparted to the experience of the Church, and more of the beauty of holiness will adorn her courts, when the Oriental world shall be converted to Christ, and Ethiopia shall stretch out her hands unto God. Our unimpassioned, taciturn, and often cloudy temperament in religion, does need an infusion of the piety which will grow up in those lands of the sun.

Such an infusion of the Oriental life-blood in the stock of our Christian experience would bring us into closer sympathy with the types of sanctification represented in the Scriptures. It would be like streams from Lebanon to our culture. We need it to render the Psalms of David, for instance, a natural expression of our devotions. We need a culture of sensibility which shall *demand* these Psalms as a medium of utterance.

We need habits of feeling, disciplined indeed, not effervescent, not mystic – but, on the other hand, not crushed, not fearful of outflow, not bereaved of speech. We need a sensitiveness to the objects of our faith, which shall *create* desire for the objects of prayer, not passionate, not devoid of self-possession, but fluent and self-forgetful in its earnestness, so that it shall have more of the grace of a child in its outgoings.

Of such an experience, intercourse with God in prayer would be the necessary expression. It could find no other so fit. Joy in that intercourse would be like the swellings of Jordan.

8: INDOLENCE IN PRAYER

'Ye said also, Behold what a weariness is it!' – MAL. 1:13

We offer many dead prayers, through *mental indolence*. This fact is often forgotten, that prayer is one of the most spiritual of the duties of religion, – spiritual as distinct from corporeal. It is the communion of a spiritual soul with a spiritual God. God calls himself the *Former*, only, of our bodies, but the *Father* of our spirits. So prayer, to be a filial intercourse with Him, must be abstract from sensation. Do we not naturally seek darkness in our devotions? Why is it that to pray with open eyes seems either heartless or ghastly? So, too, do we seek stillness and solitude. Only a Pharisee can pray at the corner of a street. A truly devout spirit learns to sing, from its own experience –

> *Blest is the tranquil hour of morn,*
> *And blest that hour of solemn eve,*
> *When, on the wings of prayer upborne,*
> *The world I leave.*

Physical enjoyment is as much a drag upon the spirit of worship as physical pain. We want nothing to remind us of our corporeal being, in these hours of communion with Him who seeth in secret. We worship One who is a Spirit. A soul caught up to the third heaven, in devout

[46]

ecstasy, cannot tell whether it be in the body or out of the body.

These well-known phenomena of prayer suggest its purely mental character. They involve, also, the need of mental exertion. 'We may pray with the intellect without praying with the heart; but we cannot pray with the heart without praying with the intellect.'

True, there is, as we shall have occasion to observe, a state of devotional culture which may render prayer habitually spontaneous, so that the mind shall be unconscious of toil in it, but shall spring to it rather as to its native and wonted atmosphere of joy. This is the reward of practised effort in all things. But who can number the struggles with a wayward spirit, which must create that high deportment in devotion?

True, there may be hours when the mind is alert, from other causes; when the fountains of the soul are unsealed by a great sorrow, or a great deliverance; when *before* we called, God has heard us, and the Spirit now helps our infirmities, so that thought is nimble, sensibility is fluent, and the mouth speaketh out of the abundance of the heart. Yet such unforeseen and gratuitous aids to mental elasticity are not the *law* of devotional life. In this, as in other things, no great blessing is given thoughtlessly, and none can be received thus. The law of blessing allies it in some sort with struggles with our own.

True, God's condescension is nowhere more conspicuous than in His hearing of prayer. No ponderous intellectual machinery is needful to its dignity; no loftiness of reasoning, no magnificence of imagery, no polish of diction, no learning, no art, no genius. In its very conception, prayer implies a *descent* of the divine mind to the homes of men; and with no design to lift men up out of the sphere of their lowliness, intellectually. Bruised reeds, smoking flax, broken hearts, dumb sufferers, the slow of speech, timid believers, tempted spirits – weakness in all its varieties – find a refuge in that thought of God, which nothing else reveals so affectingly as the gift of prayer, that He is a very *present* help in time of trouble. He whom the heaven of heavens cannot contain, 'has come down and placed Himself in the centre of the little circle of human ideas and affections,' as if for the purpose of making our 're-ligion always the homestead of common feelings.' It has been debated by philosophers, whether prayer be not of the nature of poetry. Yet poetry has seldom attempted to describe prayer; and, when it has done so, what is the phraseology in which it has spoken to our hearts most convinc-ingly? Is it that of magnificent and transcendental speech? No, it portrays prayer to us as only –

The motion of a hidden fire
That trembles in the breast –

as the mere 'burden of a sigh,' the 'falling of a tear,' 'the upward glancing of an eye,' — 'the simplest form of speech' on 'infant lips.'

All this is true, and no idea of the intellectuality of prayer should be entertained which conflicts with this. But we degrade the dignity of God's condescension, if we abuse His indulgence of our weakness to an encouragement of our indolence. Must we not wince under the rebuke of the preacher at Golden Grove: 'Can we expect that our sins can be washed by a lazy prayer? We should not dare to throw away our prayers so, like fools!'?[1]

Coleridge, in his later manhood, expressed his sorrow at having written so shallow a sentiment on the subject of prayer, as that contained in one of his youthful poems, in which, speaking of God, he had said —

Of whose all-seeing eye
Aught to demand were impotence of mind.

This sentiment he so severely condemned, that he said he thought the act of praying to be, in its most perfect form, the very highest *energy* of which the human heart was capable. The large majority of worldly men, and of learned men, he pronounced incapable of executing his ideal of prayer.

Many scriptural representations of the idea of devotion come up fully to this mark. The prayer

[1] Jeremy Taylor.

of a righteous man, that availeth much, which our English Bible so infelicitously describes as 'effectual, fervent,' is in the original an *'energetic'* prayer, a *'working'* prayer. Some conception of the inspired thought in the epithet may be derived from the fact, that the same word is elsewhere used to intensify the description of the power of the Holy Spirit in a renewed heart. Thus: 'According to the power that *worketh* in us' – the power that *energizes* us in a holy life; such is the inspired idea of a good man's prayer.

What else is the force of the frequent conjunction of 'watching' and 'praying,' in the scriptural style of exhortation to the duties of the closet? Thus: 'Watch *and* pray' 'Watch *unto* prayer' 'Praying always *and* watching' 'Continue in prayer *and* watch.' There is no mental lassitude, no self-indulgence here. It was a lament of the prophet over the degeneracy of God's people: 'None *stirreth himself up* to take hold on thee.' Paul exhorts the Romans to '*strive* together with him in their prayers'; and commends an ancient preacher to the confidence of the Colossians, as one who '*laboured fervently* in prayers.' There is no droning or drawling effort here.

Indeed, what need have we of more significant teaching on this point than our own experience? Setting aside as exceptional, emergencies in which God condescends to our incapacity of great mental exertion, do we not habitually feel the need of such exertion in our devotions? Is not even a painful effort of intellect often needful to recall our minds from secular engagements, and to give us vivid thoughts of God and of eternity? I do not assume that this *ought* to be so, or need be; I speak of what *is*, in the ordinary life of Christians.

Prayer can have no intelligent fervour, unless the objects of our faith are represented with some degree of *vividness*, in our conceptions of them. But this is a process of intellect. As we must have clear thought before we can have intelligent feeling, so must we have vivid thought before we can have profound feeling. But this, I repeat, is a process of intellect.

Yet, do we not often come to the hour and place of prayer, burdened by an exhausted body; with intellect stupified by the absorption of its forces in the plans, the toils, the perplexities, the disappointments, the irritations of the day? How wearily do we often drag this great earthen world behind us, into the presence of God! Is not our first petition, often, an ejaculation for the ornament of a meek and quiet spirit? But, in such a state of body and of mind, to acquire impressive conceptions of God and of eternity is an intellectual change. I do not affirm that a state of intellect is all that is involved here; but intellectual change is indispensable; and it requires exertion.

On this topic, what can the man do that cometh after the king? Let us hear Jeremy Taylor once more. His description of a good man's prayer, though well known, one can never outgrow.

'Prayer is the peace of our spirit, the stillness of our thoughts, the evenness of our recollection, the seat of our meditation, the rest of our cares, and the calm of our tempest. Prayer is the issue of a quiet mind, of untroubled thoughts; it is the daughter of charity and the sister of meekness. He that prays to God with . . . a troubled and discomposed spirit, is like him that retires into a battle to meditate, and sets up his closet in the outquarters of an army, and chooses a frontier garrison to be wise in.

'For so have I seen a lark rising from his bed of grass, and soaring upwards, singing as he rises, and hopes to get to heaven, and climb above the clouds; but the poor bird was beaten back by the loud sighings of an eastern wind, and his motion made irregular and inconstant, descending more at every breath of the tempest than it could recover by the libration and frequent weighing of his wings, till the little creature was forced to sit down and pant, and stay till the storm was over; and then it made a prosperous flight, and did rise and sing, as if it had learned music and motion from an angel, as he passed some time through the air, about his ministries here below.

'So is the prayer of a good man. When his

affairs have required business, . . . his duty met
with infirmities of a man, . . . and the instrument
became stronger than the prime agent, and
raised a tempest, and overruled the man; and
then his prayer was broken, and his thoughts
were troubled, and his words went up towards a
cloud, and his thoughts pulled them back again,
and made them without intention; and the good
man sighs for his infirmity, but must be content
to lose his prayer; and he must recover it when
. . . his spirit is becalmed, made even as the brow
of Jesus, and smooth like the heart of God; and
then it ascends to heaven upon the wings of the
holy dove, and dwells with God, till it returns,
like the useful bee, loaden with a blessing and the
dew of heaven.'

9: IDOLATRY IN PRAYER

'Ye have brought that which was torn, and the lame, and the sick. Should I accept this of your hand?' – MAL. 1:13

Our mental indolence may poison the very fountain of prayer. Are we not often reminded of our need of an effort of intellect, to enable us to realize to ourselves the personality of God, and to address to Him the language of supplication, as if to a friend who is invisibly with us? What is left of prayer, if these two things are abstracted from it – a sense of the personal *presence* and of the personal *friendship* of God? 'He that cometh unto God, must believe that he *is*, and that he is a *rewarder*.' Subtract these from our ideal in prayer, and all that remains the Polish peasant possessed, when he strung his prayers upon a windmill, and counted so many to the credit side of his conscience with every turn of the wheel.

A plain man once said: 'Before my conversion, when I prayed in the presence of others, I prayed to *them*; when I prayed in secret, I prayed to *myself*; but now I pray to *God*.' But your experience has doubtless taught you, long before this time, that one of the most difficult things involved in an act of devotion, is to secure to it this reality of intercourse between the soul and a present friend.

Does it cost us no effort to feel, in the silence and solitude of the closet, the truthfulness of language like this? – perhaps we are sometimes assisted by uttering it audibly – 'God is here, within these walls; before me, behind me, on my right hand, on my left hand. He who fills immensity has come down to me here. I am now about to bow at His feet, and *speak* to Him. He will hear the very words I utter. I may pour forth my desires before Him, and not one syllable from my lips shall escape His ear. I may speak to Him as I would to the dearest friend I have on earth, whose hand I should grasp, and whose eye I should watch, and in the changes of whose speaking countenance I should read the interest which he felt in my story. Yes, I am about to speak to God, though I do not see Him, no image of Him aids my vision or my faith; though I do not hear His footfall around me; He is not in the wind, nor in the earthquake, nor in the fire. Yet He is here as truly as if clothed in a refulgent body, and these eyes could look upon Him, and these ears could hear the sound of His tread.'

> *Jesus, these eyes have never seen*
> *That radiant form of thine!*
> *The veil of sense hangs dark between*
> *Thy blessed face and mine!*
>
> *I see thee not, I hear thee not,*
> *Yet art thou oft with me;*
> *And earth hath ne'er so dear a spot*
> *As where I meet with thee.*

In this manner, to feel the reality of God's spiritual presence, and then to speak the language of adoration, confession, petition, thanksgiving, with a *continuous* sense of its being, as Chalmers longed to feel it, an actual interchange between ourselves and God, a real *conference* of friends – this, surely, is not at all times, in all states of the body, in all moods of sensibility, under all varieties of circumstances, natural to fallen minds like ours. It is not a state of mind to which, without culture, without discipline in Christian life, we spring spontaneously, involuntarily, as we spring to conscious thinking when we wake from sleep. A process of intellect is involved in it which demands exertion.

The difficulty is that which idolatry was invented to meet, by furnishing an image of God to aid the mind; that is, by giving it an object of sense, to relieve it from the labour of forming the conception of a spiritual Deity.

Is it not evident, then, what effect must be produced upon our devotional hours, if we squander them, through a habit of intellectual indolence? It has been said that we are all born idolaters. We truly are very like idolaters in indolent prayers. Pursue this thought, for a moment, into the details of individual experience, and let us have courage to look the evil in the face, and call it by its right name; for this is a matter which, to be felt as it deserves, needs to be permitted to pierce to the most secret habits of the closet.

Imagine, then, that you go to your place of retirement reluctantly, listlessly. Your mind, perhaps, is in a state of reaction from the excitements of the day. You are indisposed to *thought* of any kind. You have no eagerness of search after God; it is not the struggling cry of your heart, 'Oh that I knew where I might find him!' From sheer reluctance to endure the labour of thinking, you neglect preparatory meditation. You read the Scriptures indolently; you do not expect, or seek for a spur to your own conceptions, in the words of inspired thinkers. Your indolent mind infects the body with its infirmity; you instinctively choose that posture in your devotions which is most tempting to physical repose.

Imagine that, in the act of prayer, your mind dreams its way through a dialect of dead words: it floats on the current of a stereotyped phraseology which once leaped with life from the lips of holy men who originated it; but some of which your memory obliges you to confess, never *had* any vitality in your own thoughts. It was never *original* with you; you have never worked it out in your own experience; you have never *lived* it; it has never forced itself into expression, as the fruit of self-knowledge or of self-conflict.

Or, imagine that you occasionally, or even habitually, pray inaudibly, because the luxuriousness of that silent thought is more facile to an indolent spirit than the labour of expressing thought with the living voice. You cannot often say, with David, 'I cried unto the Lord with my *voice*; with my *voice* unto the Lord did I make my supplication.' You do not pause, and struggle with yourself, and gird up your loins like a man, and ejaculate a cry for divine aid, in the mastery of thoughts which wander like the fool's eyes. And you close your prayer with a formula which touches the very soul of faith, and hope, and love, and all that is grand and mysterious and eternal in redemption – a formula hallowed by centuries of prayer; yet, in uttering it, when you say, 'For Christ's sake, Amen,' your mind is not conscious of a single definite, affecting thought, of either the history or the meaning of that language.

Imagine this as a scene of real life in the closet. *Is* this a caricature of some possible modes of secret devotion? And if it is not, is it marvellous that *such* devotion should be *afflicted* with a want of enjoyment of the divine presence? 'Should I accept *this* of your hand? saith the Lord.'

The truth is, that an indulgence of sluggishness of mind is sometimes the secret sin of good men. It is the iniquity which they regard in their hearts, and because of which God will not hear them. Mental ease is a refined and seductive idol, which often beguiles men who have too much Christian principle, or too much delicacy of nature, or too much prudence of self-control, or it may be too much pride of character, to fall into a physical vice.

When good men are ensnared in this sleek idolatry, before the decline of old age or the infirmities of disease render rest a necessity, God often breaks in upon it with the blows of His hard hand. He fights against it 'with battles of shaking,' and in part with the design of recalling His mistaken friends into closer communion with Himself. He thwarts their plans of life. He sends trouble to plague them. He knocks out from under them the props of their comfort. He does this, in part, for the sake of startling their torpid minds, and thus reaching their stagnant hearts, by giving them something to think of, which they feel they *must* make the subject of living, agonizing prayer.

10: CONTINUANCE IN PRAYER

'Could ye not watch with me one hour?' – MATT. 26:40

We are often in a *religious hurry* in our devotions. How much *time* do we spend in them daily? Can it not be easily reckoned in minutes?

Probably many of us would be discomposed by an arithmetical estimate of our communion with God. It might reveal to us the secret of much of our apathy in prayer, because it might disclose how little we desire to be alone with God. We might learn from such a computation, that Augustine's idea of prayer, as 'the measure of love,' is not very flattering to us. We do not grudge time given to a privilege which we love.

Why should we expect to enjoy a duty which we have no time to enjoy? Do we enjoy anything which we do in a hurry? Enjoyment presupposes something of mental leisure. How often do we say of a pleasure, 'I wanted more *time* to enjoy it to my heart's content.' But of all employments, none can be more dependent on 'time for it,' than *stated* prayer.

Fugitive acts of devotion, to be of high value, must be sustained by other approaches to God, deliberate, premeditated, regular, which shall be to those acts like the abutments of a suspension bridge to the arch that spans the river. It will never do to be in desperate haste in laying such foundations. This *thoughtful* duty, this *spiritual* privilege, this foretaste of *incorporeal* life, this communion with an *unseen* Friend, can you expect to enjoy it as you would a repartee or a dance?

In the Royal Gallery at Dresden may be often seen a group of connoisseurs, who sit for hours before a single painting. They walk around those halls and corridors, whose walls are so eloquent with the triumphs of art, and they come back and pause again before that one masterpiece. They go away, and return the next day; and again the first and the last object which charms their eye, is that canvas on which genius has pictured more of beauty than on any other in the world. Weeks are spent every year in the study of that one work of Raphael. Lovers of art cannot enjoy it to the full, till they have made it their own, by prolonged communion with its matchless forms. Says one of its admirers: 'I could spend an hour every day, for years, upon that assemblage of human, and angelic, and divine ideals, and on the last day of the last year discover some new beauty, and a new joy.'

I have seen men standing in the street, before an engraving of that gem of the Dresden Gallery, a longer time than a good man will sometimes devote to his evening prayer. Yet, what thoughts, what ideals of grace, can genius express in a painting, demanding time for their appreciation and enjoyment, like those great thoughts of God, of heaven, of eternity, which the soul needs to conceive *vividly*, in order to know the blessedness of prayer? What conceptions can art imagine of the 'Divine Child,' which can equal in spirituality the thoughts which one needs to entertain of Christ in the 'prayer of faith'? We cannot hope, commonly, to *spring* into possession of such thoughts in the twinkling of an eye.

Prayer, as we have observed, is an act of *friendship* also. It is intercourse; an act of trust, of hope, of love – all prompting to *interchange* between the soul and an infinite, spiritual Friend. We all need prayer, if for no other purpose, for this which we so aptly call *communion* with God.

Robert Burns lamented that he could not 'pour out his inmost soul without reserve to any human being, without danger of one day repenting his confidence.' He commenced a journal of his own mental history, 'as a substitute,' he said, 'for a confidential friend.' He would have some thing 'which he could record *himself* in,' without peril of having his confidence betrayed. We all need prayer, as a means of such intercourse with a Friend who will be true to us.

Zinzendorf, when a boy, used to write little notes to the Saviour, and throw them out of the window, hoping that He would find them. Later in life, so strong was his faith in the friendship of Christ, and in his own need of that friendship as a daily solace, that once, when travelling, he sent back his companion that he might converse more freely with 'the Lord,' with whom he spoke audibly.

So do we all need friendly converse with Him whom our souls love. 'He alone is a thousand companions; He alone is a world of friends. That man never knew what it was to be familiar with God, who complains of the want of friends while God is with him.'

But who can originate such conceptions of God as are necessary to the enjoyment of His friendship in prayer, without *time* for thought, for self-collection, for concentration of soul? Momentary devotion, if genuine, must presuppose the *habit* of studious prayer.

We have portraits of deceased friends, before which we love to sit by the hour, striving to recall the living features which are so feebly portrayed there, and to resuscitate the *history* of expression on those countenances in life, which no art could fix on canvas, and to which our own memory is becoming treacherous. Have we never struggled with the twilight, to make those loved but flitting expressions live again?

Yet, have we any more vivid or indelible conceptions of God, 'whom no man hath seen at any time'? How can we expect to enjoy a sense of the friendship of the present Saviour, if we never linger in the twilight, to freshen and intensify our thoughts of Him? Does He never speak to *us* that plaintive reproof, 'Could ye not watch with me *one* hour?'

A very *busy* Christian says, 'This is a cloistral piety which demands much time for secret prayer.' No, not that! But, on the other hand, it is not a piety which, in its recoil from the monastery, is heedless of the look of *business* in *devotion*, which is expressed by the words, 'Enter into thy closet and *shut thy door*'; and of the scriptural stress upon *perseverance* in prayer; and of the inspired idea of *fasting* and prayer; and of the historic argument from the *example* of eminent saints, both of biblical and of later times.

Who ever knew an eminently holy man who did not spend much of his time in prayer? Did ever a man exhibit *much* of the *spirit* of prayer, who did not devote much time to his closet? Whitefield says, 'Whole days and weeks have I spent prostrate on the ground, in silent or vocal prayer.' 'Fall upon your knees, and *grow* there,' is the language of another, who knew that whereof he affirmed. These, in spirit, are but specimens of a feature in the experience of eminent piety, which is absolutely uniform.

It has been said that no great work in literature or in science was ever wrought by a man who did not love solitude. We may lay it down as an elemental principle of religion, that no large growth in holiness was ever gained by one who did not *take* time to be often long *alone with God*.

'Holiness,' says Dr. Cudworth, is 'something of God, wherever it is. It is an efflux from Him, and lives in Him; as the sunbeams, although they gild this lower world, and spread their golden wings over us, yet they are not so much here where they shine, as in the sun from whence they flow.' Such a possession of the idea of God we never gain but from still hours. For such holy joy in God, we must have much of the spirit of Him who rose up a great while before day, and departed into a solitary place and prayed, and who continued all night in prayer; 'the morning star finding Him where the evening star had left Him.'

11: FRAGMENTARY PRAYER

'A devout man, one that prayed alway.' – ACTS 10:2.

We miss very much devotional joy, by the neglect of *fragmentary* prayer. In the intervals which separate periodical seasons of devotion, we need a habit of offering up brief ejaculatory expressions of devout feeling. The morning and the evening sacrifice depend very much upon these interspersed offerings, as these in return are dependent on those. Communion with God in both, is assisted by linking the 'set times' together by a chain of heavenward thoughts and aspirations, in the breaks which occur in our labours and amusements. Sunrise and sunset may attract our *attention* more strongly than the succession of golden rays between them, but who can say that they are more cheering? It is not often that a day wholly clouded lies between two clear twilights.

Prayer, as we have seen, is, in the highest conception of it, a *state* rather than an *act*. A full fruition of its benefits depends on a *continuity* of its influences. Reduce it to two isolated experiments daily, and separate these by long blank hours in which the soul has no glimpse of God for its refreshment, and how can prayer be other than a toil, and often a drudgery?

We come to the eventide with the impression of the morning watch all obliterated; probably with a conscience burdened by accumulations of sin upon an ungoverned spirit through the day. We feel that we must make a new start every time we seek God's presence. Our sense of spiritual progress is lost. Sinning and repenting is all our life; we do not have holy force enough to get beyond repentance in our devotion. Our prayers, instead of being, as they should be, advancing steps, are like the steps of a treadmill. Human law has abandoned this, even as a punishment for felons; why should one whom Christ has made free inflict it upon himself?

We need, then, something that shall make our prayerful hours support each other – the morning tributary to the evening, and the evening to the morning. Nothing else can do this so naturally as the habit of ejaculatory prayer. The *spirit* of prayer may run along the line of such a habit through a lifetime. So, one may live in a *state* of prayer, 'a devout man that prays always.'

Not only does this habit of fragmentary prayer contribute to a lofty, devotional spirit, but such a spirit demands it for its own indulgence.

It is characteristic of minds which are aspiring in their piety, and which have begun to reap the reward of arduous devotional culture, to be habitually conversant with God. Such minds are constantly *looking up*. In the very midst of earthly toils, they seize moments of relief, to spring up to the eminences of meditation, where they love to dwell. In the discharge of duties

most unfriendly to holy joy, they are apt to experience a buoyancy of impulse towards a heavenly
plane of thought, which it may even require a
power of self-denial to keep down.

Critics have observed, that in the apostolic
epistles, doxologies are sometimes imbedded in
passages of remonstrance and of warning. It
would seem that the apostolic mind came down
unwillingly, or from a sense of duty only, to deal
with the sins and weaknesses of earth; and was
on the watch for chances to rise, like a bird let
loose, though but for a moment, into the upper air.

Such is the nature of holiness. Being *from*
God, it is ever seeking to revert to its source.
The heavier the pressure of a mundane life upon
it, the stronger is the force of its compressed
aspirations. Such pressure is like that of the
atmosphere on water, which seeks, through
crevices in its enclosure, the level of its fountain.
A spirit like this, I repeat, will *demand* the habit
of fragmentary prayer for its own holy indulgence;
and will demand it with an importunity proportioned to the superincumbent weight of
earthly cares.

The providence of God, also, contemplates
these impulses as a counterpart to certain of its
own procedures.

Under the laws of providence, life is a probation; probation is a succession of temptations;
temptations are emergencies; and for emergencies

we need the preparation and the safeguard of prayer.

We have duties which are perilous. We meet surprises of evil. We struggle with a wily adversary. We feel perplexities of conscience, in which holy decision depends on the mind we bring to them. We encounter disappointments which throw us back from our hopes rudely. We have difficult labours, in which we sometimes come to a 'dead-lock'; we do not know what to do. We have an *unknown* experience opening upon us every hour. We are like travellers in a fog, who cannot see an arm's-length before them. Providence is thus continually calling for the aids of prayer; and in a soul which is keen in its vigilance, prayer will be continually responsive to providences, often anticipative of them.

The methods of the Holy Spirit, also, presuppose the value of these fragmentary devotions. God often secretly inclines a Christian's heart to engage in them.

Are there not, in the lives of us all, moments when, without the formality of retirement to the closet, we feel *disposed* to pray? We are conscious of special attraction towards God. Perhaps with no obvious reason for 'looking up' now rather than an hour ago, we *do* look up. 'We feel just like praying.' It is as if we heard heavenly voices saying, 'Come up hither.'

There is often a beautiful *alliance* between

providence and grace, in these experiences. A Christian who will be studious of his own history, will probably discover that often the *occasions* for such fragmentary communings with God follow hard upon these secret incitements to them. Emergencies come soon for which they are needed. The Holy Spirit has anticipated them, and sought to fore-arm us. Providence and grace thus hover over us, not far asunder.

In this view, those biblical exhortations to prayer, which men have sometimes deemed extravagant, are transparently rational: 'Continue* in prayer', 'Continue *instant* in prayer', 'Pray *without ceasing*', 'Men ought *always* to pray', '*Rejoice* in the Lord *alway*'! Such exhortations contemplate a state, not insulated acts of prayer. They *fit in* well to the system of things in which we are living; for that system seems, on all sides of it, to pre-suppose just this continuity of unpremeditated ejaculations, joining together our stated seasons of devotion.

No Christian, then, can afford to be frugal of prayer, in the intervals of daily business and amusement. Enjoyment of *all* communion with God must be impaired by the loss of these little tributaries. A Christian's life, so conducted, must languish as a tree does whose fibrous roots are stripped off, leaving only its truncal roots, possibly only a tap-root, for its nourishment. That Christian is hoping against impossibilities, who thinks to enjoy a life of intercourse with God in any such way.

We are opposing God's method of working, if our life has a tendency to incapacitate us for the enjoyment of prayer *at all times*. If by needless excess of worldly cares; if by inordinate desires, which render it impossible for us to accomplish our objects in life *without* such excess of care; if by frivolous habits; if by the reading of infidel or effeminate literature; if by an indolent life; if by any self-indulgence in physical regimen – if, I say, we render the habit of fragmentary prayer impracticable or unnatural to us, *we are crossing the methods of God's working*. Something has gone wrong, *is* going wrong, in the life of him who finds himself thus estranged from filial freedom with God.

Such a Christian must, sooner or later, be brought back to Christ, and must begin life anew. He will come back heavy laden and in tears. No words express more becomingly the wail of his spirit, whenever he comes to his right mind, than the plaint of Cowper –

Oh, for a closer walk with God!

In the vestibule of St. Peter's, at Rome, is a doorway, which is walled up and marked with a cross. It is opened but four times in a century. On Christmas Eve, once in twenty-five years, the pope approaches it in princely state, with the retinue of cardinals in attendance, and begins the demolition of the door, by striking it three times with a silver hammer. When the passage is opened, the multitude pass into the nave of the cathedral, and up to the altar, by an avenue which the majority of them never entered thus before, and never will enter thus again.

Imagine that the way to the throne of grace were like the *Porta Santa*, inaccessible, save once in a quarter of a century, on the twenty-fifth of December, and then only with august solemnities, conducted by great dignitaries in a 'holy' city. Conceive that it were now ten years since you, or I, or any other sinner had been *permitted* to pray; and that fifteen long years must drag themselves away before we could venture again to approach God; and that, at the most, we could not hope to pray more than two or three times in a lifetime! With what solicitude we should wait for the coming of that holy day! We should lay our plans of life, select our homes, build our houses, choose our professions, form our friendships, with reference to a *pilgrimage* in that twenty-fifth year. We should reckon time by the openings of that sacred door, as epochs. No other one thought would engross so much of our lives, or kindle our sensibilities so intensely, as the thought of prayer. It would be of more significance to us than the thought of death is now. It would multiply our trepidations at the thought of dying. Fear would grow to horror, at the idea of dying before that year of jubilee. No other question would give us such tremors of anxiety as these would excite: 'How many years now to *the* time of prayer? How many months? How many weeks? How many days? Shall we live to see it? Who can tell?'

Yet, on that great day, amidst an innumerable throng, in a courtly presence, within sight and hearing of stately rites, *what would prayer be worth to us?* Who would value it in comparison with those still moments, that

Secret silence of the mind,

in which we now can 'find God,' *every* day and *every* where? That day would be more like the day of judgment to us, than like the sweet minutes of converse with 'our Father,' which we may now have every hour. We should appreciate this privilege of *hourly* prayer, if it were once taken from us. Should we not?

Still with thee, O my God,
I would desire to be;
By day, by night, at home, abroad,
I would be still with thee!

With thee amid the crowd
That throngs the busy mart —
To hear thy voice 'mid clamour loud,
Speak softly to my heart!

[73]

12: AID OF THE HOLY SPIRIT
IN PRAYER

'The Spirit also helpeth our infirmities.' – ROM. 8:26

Langour may be the penalty of *egotism* in prayer. No other infirmity is so subtle, or so corrosive to devotion, as that of an overweening consciousness of self. It is possible that an intense self-conceit should flaunt itself in the forms of devoutness.

To a right-minded man, some of the most astonishing passages in the Bible are the mysterious declarations and hints of the *residence* of the Holy Spirit in a human soul. We must stand in awe before any just conception of the meaning of such voices as these: 'The Spirit of God dwelleth in you', 'God dwelleth in us', 'Ye are the temple of God', 'Your body is the temple of the Holy Ghost', 'Full of the Holy Ghost', 'Filled with all the fulness of God', 'Praying in the Holy Ghost', 'With all prayer in the Spirit', 'The Spirit itself maketh intercession for us.'

But the mysteriousness of such language should not surprise us. Its mystery is only the measure of its depth. It is the reality which it expresses that is amazing. Let us not fritter it away by shallow interpretations. While, on the one hand, we are under no necessity of blinking the truth of the intense activity of the soul in any holy experience, on the other hand, we must discern in such phraseology the *greater* intensity of the

Holy Spirit's action *in* a holy mind. The existence of the mind is no more a reality than this indwelling of God.

What then is prayer, as seen in *perspective*, with this doctrine of 'the Spirit'? Is it merely the dialect of helplessness? Is it only, as Paley defines it, the expression of want? Is it nothing but the lament of poverty, or the moan of suffering, or the cry of fear? Is it simply the trust of weakness in strength, the leaning of ignorance upon wisdom, the dependence of guilt upon mercy? It is all these, but more. A holy prayer is the Spirit of God speaking through the infirmities of a human soul –

God's breath in man, returning to his birth.

We scarcely utter hyperbole in saying that prayer is the Divine Mind communing with itself, through finite wants, through the woes of helplessness, through the clinging instincts of weakness. On this side of the judgment, no other conception of the presence of God is so profound as that which is realized in our souls every time we offer a genuine prayer. God is then not only *with* us, but *within* us.

That was human nature in honest dismay at its own guilt, in which the children of Israel said to Moses, 'Speak thou with us, and we will hear; let not God speak with us lest we die.' That was an adventurous trustfulness which could

[75]

enable the monk of Mount St. Agnes to say of this language, 'I pray not in this manner; no, Lord, I pray not so; but with Samuel I entreat, "Speak, Lord, for thy servant heareth." Do thou, therefore, O Lord my God, speak to my soul lest I die.' But what is the sacredness of God's speaking *to* us, in comparison of the more awful thought of His speaking *within* us! Yet this is prayer. 'Know ye not that ye are the temple of God?'

It is obvious, then, that the loss of much joy in prayer may be attributed to some form of dishonour done to the Holy Spirit, in either the intent or the manner of our devotions. The Spirit sternly refuses to become a participant in any act which disparages Him, and exalts in the heart of the worshipper the idea of self. A profound Christian truth may be clothed in the language of a heathen proverb: 'A divine Spirit is within us, who treats us as He is treated by us.'

We may offer our supplications with no penetrating sense of the *necessity* of supernatural aid. There may be no childlike consciousness of infirmity which should lead us to cry out for help. The inspired words, often on our lips, may seldom come from the depth of our hearts: 'We know not what we should pray for as we ought.' We make prayer itself one of the standard subjects of prayer; yet on what theme do our devotions more frequently degenerate into routine than on this?

Have we a sense of indigence when we ask for the indwelling of God in our souls? Have we such a sense of need of it, as we have of the need of air when we are gasping with faintness? It is the law of divine blessing, that want comes before wealth, hunger before a feast. We must experience the necessity in order to appreciate the reality.

Have we desires in prayer which we feel unable to utter without the aid of God? Dr. Payson said that he pitied the Christian who had no longings at the throne of grace which he could not clothe in language. There may be a silent disavowal of our need of the Holy Ghost in the very act in which we seek His energy. The lips may honour Him, but the heart may say, 'What have I to do with Thee?'

We may dishonour the Holy Spirit by irreverent *speech* in prayer. The Spirit can indite no other than reverent words. Where do we find, in the Scriptures, an unhallowed familiarity of communion with God? Only at the gathering of the sons of God, at which 'Satan came also among them.' It required the effrontery of an evil spirit to talk to God as to an equal.

The consciousness of divine friendship in devotion, so far from being impaired, is deepened by holy veneration. The purest and most lasting human friendships are permeated with an element of reverence; much more this friendship of a man with God. Moses, with whom God spoke 'as a

man with his friend,' was the man who said, 'I
exceedingly fear and quake.' Abraham was called
'the friend of God'; yet his favourite posture in
prayer was prostration. He 'fell on his face, and
God talked with him.' Angels, too, veil their
faces in any service which approximates to the
nature of prayer.

> Lowly reverent
> Towards either throne they bow, and to the
>   ground,
> With solemn adoration, down they cast
> Their crowns, inwove with amarant and gold.

Even He who could say to His Father, 'I know
that thou always hearest me,' we are told, 'was
heard in that he *feared*.'

What, other than solemn mockery, can that
devotion be which clothes itself in pert speech?
The heart which is moved in healthy pulsations
of sympathy with the promptings of the Holy
Ghost indulges in no such gasconade. It is not
boisterous and rude of tongue, lifting itself up to
'talk saucily to God.' It is emptied of self, because
it is filled with the fulness of God. Therefore it
rejoices with joy unspeakable.

We may disparage the Holy Spirit by a *querulous* devotion. Self-sufficiency is impatient when it
is rebuffed; scarcely less so in intercourse with
God than in intercourse with men. Complaint
that prayer is not answered immediately, or in the

specific thing we pray for, proves that the Spirit has not 'helped our infirmities' in that prayer. We have not sought His aid, nor desired it. He prompts only submissive petitions, patient desires, a willingness to *wait* on God quietly and self-forgetfully.

A Hottentot beats his idol when he fails in his supplications. The people of Naples are frenzied with rage when the miracle of the 'liquefaction' does not appear at the festival of San Gennaro. How far is that Christian elevated above these, in possession of the 'fruit of the Spirit,' whose heart mutters hard thoughts of God at the delay or the refusal of an answer to his prayers? Such devotion is intensely selfish, however it may be glossed by the refinements of devout speech.

We may be false to the moving of the Holy Spirit by a diseased inspection of our own minds in the act of communion with God. Self-examination is a suitable preliminary or after-thought to prayer, but is no *part* of it. Devotion is most thoroughly objective, in respect of the motives which induce its presence. It is won into exercise by attractions from without, not forced into being by internal commotions. It is an outgoing, not a seething of sensibility. The suppliant looks upward and around beyond himself; and devout affection grows in intensity with the distance which he penetrates, as the eye grows keen with far seeing. The Spirit invites to no other than such expansive devotion. We are never more like Christ than in prayers of intercession. In the most lofty devotion we become unconscious of self.

Joy too, has, from its very nature, the same objective origin. It springs from fountains out of ourselves. It comes to us; we do not originate it, we do not gain it by searching. We are never jubilant in *thinking* of our joy. Our happiness is an *incident* of which, as an object of thought, we are unconscious. Divine influence is adjusted to this law of our minds; it seeks to bless us by leading us out of self into great thoughts of God.

Hence, one of the most delusive methods of crossing the will of the Holy Spirit, is that habit of mental introversion in prayer, which corresponds to 'morbid anatomy' in medical science. The heart, instead of flowing outward and upward at the bidding of the Spirit, turns in upon itself, and dissects its own emotions, and studies its own *symptoms* of piety. Any kindlings of joy in the soul are quenched by being made the subject of morbid analysis.

'There are anatomists of piety,' says Isaac Taylor, 'who destroy all the freshness of faith, and hope, and charity, by immuring themselves, night and day, in the infected atmosphere of their own bosoms.' Andrew Fuller has recorded of himself, that he found no permanent relief from melancholy, in his early religious life, till his heart outgrew the pettiness of his own sorrows, through his zeal in the work of foreign missions. We may often be sensible that the 'teachings of the Spirit' in our hearts are of just this character. They prompt away from ourselves. 'Look up, look abroad,' is the interpretation of them. 'Come away from thyself; pray for something out of thine own soul; be generous in thine intercession; so shall thy peace be as a river.'

Have you never observed how entirely devoid is the Lord's Prayer of any material which can tempt to this subtle self-inspection in the act of devotion? It is full of an *outflowing* of thought and of emotion towards great objects of desire, great necessities, and great perils. 'After this manner, therefore, pray ye.'

13: REALITY OF CHRIST IN
PRAYER

'We have an advocate with the Father.' – 1 JOHN 2:1

Christians sometimes offer *heathen* prayers. The lifelessness of devotion may often be attributable to the want of a cordial recognition of *Christ* as the medium of access to the throne of grace. Prayer, in the divine plan of things, has but one avenue: 'No man cometh unto the Father but by me.' Whoever slights Christ in devotion, 'climbeth up some other way.'

The central idea in the Christian theory of prayer is that of *privilege* gained by *mediation*. The language of Christian faith is, 'I am permitted to pray because of the merits of another; I do not deserve to pray, I cannot claim to pray, I have no *right* to pray, but by Christ's permission.' The doctrine of prayer, as a doctrine of nature, is but a fragmentary truth. In its fulness it is a Christian peculiarity. The fact of an atonement is its foundation. The person of a Redeemer is the nucleus of its history.

One of the grounds on which the necessity of a revelation rests is that, by the teachings of nature, we have no *clear* right to pray – no right which satisfies a guilty conscience. Philosophy has often taught men that prayer is impiety. To an awakened conscience, nature seems to shut man in to the solitude of his own forebodings. In its dim light, prayer and sacrifice grope hand in hand as the blind leading the blind. The right of either to existence is only a presumed right. Faith in efficacy of either staggers whenever the soul is shaken by remorse, or philosophy approaches the Christian conception of sin.

Not till Christ is revealed does prayer *settle* itself as an undoubted fact; and then it is as a privilege only, and as a device of *mediatorial* government. We *may* pray, *'for Christ's sake.'* This is the Christian theory of prayer, and this is the whole of it.

Now it is not difficult to see that one may pray with no adequate appreciation of this mediatorial element in the ground-work of devotion. A man may habitually pray with no such cordiality of soul towards Christ as is becoming to a suppliant whose only right of prayer is a right purchased by atoning blood.

Is it unusual for a Christian mind to be thus heedless of Christ in devotion? Practical heresy of this kind may nestle side by side with irre-proachable orthodoxy. A creed and a faith, even upon a truth so vital, are, by no means, of neces-sity one. The very soundness of the creed may shelter the decay of the faith. We may 'profess and call ourselves Christians,' and yet may every day approach God as a converted heathen would, who had never heard of Christ. The general mercy of God may be the foundation of all the hopefulness, all the trust, all the fervour we really feel in prayer, while not a thought occurs to us of Christ as the ground of that mercy. We may pray, then, as perhaps Socrates and Plato prayed.

But what an Arctic temperature does such prayer suggest to one who can say, with Simeon, 'Mine eyes have seen thy salvation'! Such devotion could do no justice to Christian truth. It could be no exponent of Christian privilege. It is no Christian prayer.

In the experience of a Christian mind, such prayer would involve a conceivable, but an impossible distinction, which expresses, perhaps, as nearly as language can describe it, the error of him who struggles with such an idea of devotion. It is, that one may approach God rather as a *good man* than as a *redeemed sinner*. This, be it repeated, is an unreal distinction in any religious life on this globe. Christian faith recognizes no other objects of God's mercy than redeemed sinners. No others are invited to hold communion with God. The invitation is to 'the world,' only because God so loved 'the world' that it is a redeemed world. That Christian struggles against impossibilities who strives to realize, in his own experience, any other than the joy of a redeemed sinner.

Yet the human heart is exceedingly tortuous in its exercises on this theme. I repeat that a neglect of Christ may lurk in our habits of feeling and may give character to our devotions, when no heresy infects the convictions of our intellect.

A distinguished divine of the last generation expressed his confidence in the faith of a Christian brother, whose soundness as a theologian had been questioned, and he gave as his reason, that he had heard that brother pray, and that he prayed as if *Christ*, as an atoning Saviour, were a reality to him, and that such a man could not be essentially heterodox. The principle was truthful; but the converse of it is not so. The experience of prayer may be founded on no more than Socrates believed, and yet the creed of the intellect may be that of the Epistle to the Romans.

We do not need to be taught for the enlightenment of our understanding; but *do* we not need that that Spirit, who shall not speak of Himself, but shall take of the things of Christ and show them unto us, should teach our *hearts* that the most profound joy in communion with God must centre in an experience of the reality of the atoning blood? In this one thought it must culminate and rest.

A divided heart on this subject cannot know the fulness of the liberty of prayer. A heart that is confused in its religious life, by a compromise of this truth, cannot. Christ, as the Atoning One, must be a reality to the soul, or prayer cannot rise to its full growth as an experience of blessedness in the friendship of God. For such blessedness, we need much of that sense of the reality of Christ which one of the early preachers of New England is said to have had upon his death-bed, when, after giving his last messages to his earthly friends, he turned and said, 'Where, now, is Jesus of Nazareth, my most intimate, most faithful friend?'

May we not often solve, with this principle, the mystery of God's disciplinary providence? 'Many are the afflictions of the righteous'; and 'wherefore,' writes one, 'but to necessitate the use of prayer as a real and efficient means of obtaining assistance in distress?' 'Lord, in trouble have they visited thee,' says another; 'they *poured out* a prayer when thy chastening was upon them.' Often to deepen our knowledge of Christ in prayer is the mission of the angel of sorrow.

The truth is that we never feel Christ to be a reality until we feel Him to be a *necessity*. Therefore, God makes us feel that necessity. He tries us here, and He tries us there. He chastises on this side, and He chastises on that side. He probes us by the disclosure of one sin, and another, and a third, which have lain rankling in our deceived hearts. He removes, one after another, the objects in which we have been seeking the repose of idolatrous affection. He afflicts us in ways which we have not anticipated. He sends upon us the chastisements which He knows we shall feel most sensitively. He pursues us when we would fain flee from His hand; and, if need be, He shakes to pieces the whole framework of our plans of life, by which we have been struggling to build together the service of God and the service of self; till, at last, He makes us feel that Christ is all that is left to us.

When we discover that, and go to Christ, conscious of our beggary in respect of everything else – wretched, and miserable, and poor, and blind and naked – we go not expecting much, perhaps not asking much. There may be hours of prostration, when we ask only for *rest*; we pray for the cessation of suffering; we seek repose from conflict with ourselves, and with God's providence. But God gives us more. He is more generous than we have dared to believe. He gives us joy; He gives us liberty; He gives us victory; He gives us a sense of self-conquest, and of union with Himself in an eternal friendship. On the basis of that single experience of Christ as a reality, because a necessity, there rises an experience of blessedness in communion with God, which prayer expresses like a revelation. Such devotion is a jubilant psalm.

14: MODERN HABITS OF PRAYER

'Draw nigh to God, and he will draw nigh to you.' —
JAS. 4:8

God only knows what are the prevailing habits of Christians of our own day, respecting the duties of the closet. On no subject is it more necessary to speak with reserve, if we would speak justly of the experience of others. Each man knows his own, and for the most part, only his own. That is not likely to be a truthful or a candid severity, which would bring sweeping accusations against the fidelity of God's people in their intercourse with Him. We should believe no such charges. They are sometimes made in a spirit which invites one to say to the censorious brother, 'Take heed to thyself; Satan hath desired to have *thee*.'

It cannot reasonably be doubted, that multitudes of Christ's followers are struggling daily to get nearer to God. Perhaps of all the recent treasures of hymnology, no other lines have thrilled so many Christian hearts, or called forth so deep a throb of sympathy as the following from one of our living poets,

Nearer, my God, to thee, —
Nearer to thee;
Even though it be a cross
That raiseth me,
Still, all my song shall be,

[88]

Nearer, my God, to thee, –
Nearer to thee!

None are more sensible of their failures in prayer than those Christians to whom these words have become a song of the heart, more precious than rubies. Yet such Christians are more successful than they seem to themselves.

It cannot be proved that the modern church – taking into account its numbers, the variety of rank, of nation, of temperament, and of opinion which it embraces, the breadth of its Christian character, and the energy of its benevolent activities – is inferior, in respect of the *spirit* of prayer, in its most scriptural and healthy forms, to the church of any other, even of apostolic times. It is often affirmed, to the discredit of the modern developments of piety; but I repeat, it cannot be proved, nor, in view of the *aggressive* revival of religion which seems to be sweeping over Protestant Christendom,[1] is it probably true. It is not the law of divine influence, to bestow *such* measure of power when and where the spirit of prayer is dying out. The law of procedure, in reference to such grand strides of progress, is rather, 'For all this will I be inquired of by the house of Israel.' The language of fidelity, then, should not be mistaken for the language of suspicion and of croaking.

Yet, this doubtless is true of the tendencies of

[1] The author refers to the years 1857–9.

[89]

our modern Christian life – that they embody
certain *centrifugal* forces, as related to a life of
solitude and stillness. Modern piety goes outward,
in duties and activities, extrinsic to a secret life
with God. It does this by an inborn instinct,
which perhaps was never more vigorous in its
operation than now. This is no evil. It is a growth,
rather, upon the usage of other ages, and it is a
salutary growth.

But, like every large, rapid growth, it involves
a peril which we cannot avoid, but which, by
wise forethought, we may encounter with safe
courage. That very obvious peril is, that the
vitality of holiness may be exhausted by inward
decay, through the want of an *increase* of its
devotional spirit, proportioned to the expansion of
its active forces. Individual experience may become shallow, for the want of meditative habits
and much communion with God.

Should this be the catastrophe of the tendencies
working in modern Christian life, centuries of
conflict and corruption must follow, by a law
fixed like gravitation. Our religious organizations
must begin soon to *settle*, like a building whose
frame is eaten through and through with the 'dry-
rot.' Activity can sustain *itself*. Withdraw the
vital force which animates and propels it and it
falls like a dead arm. We cannot, then, too keenly
feel, each one for himself, that a still and secret
life with God must energize all holy duty, as

vigour in every fibre of the body must come from the strong, calm, faithful beat of the heart.

To one who is conscious of defect in his own piety, respecting the friendship of the soul with God, there will be great aptness and beauty in the appeal of a foreign preacher: 'Why fleest thou from solitude? Why dost thou shun the lonely hour? Why passeth thy life away like the feast of the drunkard? Why is it that to many of you there cometh not, through the whole course of the week, a single hour for self-meditation? You go through life like dreaming men. Ever among mankind, and never with yourselves. . . . You have torn down the cloister, but why have you not erected it within your own hearts? Lo, my brother, if thou wouldst seek out the *still hour*, only a single one every day; and if thou wouldst meditate on the love which called thee into being, which hath overshaded thee all the days of thy life with blessing, or else by mournful experiences hath admonished and corrected thee, – this would be to draw near to thy God. Thus wouldst thou take Him by the hand. But whenever, in ceaseless dissipation of heart, thou goest astray, the sea of the divine blessing shall surround thee on all sides and yet thy soul shall be athirst. Wilt thou draw near to God? . . . Then seek the STILL HOUR.'